Mighty
CARS

IAN GRAHAM

W
FRANKLIN WATTS
LONDON • SYDNEY

An Appleseed Editions book

First published in 2006 by Franklin Watts
338 Euston Road, London NW1 3BH

Franklin Watts Australia
Hachette Children's Books
Level 17/207 Kent St, Sydney, NSW 2000

© 2006 Appleseed Editions

Appleseed Editions Ltd,
Well House, Friars Hill, Guestling, East Sussex, TN35 4ET

Created by Q2A Creative
Editor: Chester Fisher
Designer: Mini Dhawan, Ashita Murgai
Picture Researcher: Ankita Kilawala

ISBN 0 7496 6748 6

Dewey Classification: 629.222

A CIP catalogue for this book is available from the British Library.

Picture credits
t=top b=bottom c=center l=left r=right
Adam Alberti: 19t, BMW: 7b, 11b, 15t, Bugatti: 12tr (above), 12tr (below), 12b, Castrol Ltd Archive: 26b, 27t,
Craftsmen Limousine: 21tl, 21tr, DaimlerChrysler: 6c, 9b, 13t, 13b, 17b, 18b, 24c, 24b,
Daniel Ingham: 23t, Dragster.com.au: 17t, General Motors: 22b, 29t,
Moller International: www.moller.com: 28b, National Motor Museum, Beaulieu: 5b, 9t, 27b,
Teemu Mottonen/teemu.net: 16b, Walter P. Reuther Library, Wayne State University: 14b,
www.motoringpicturelibrary.com: 8t, 10c, 25t, cover, www.usmc.mil: 19b

Printed in Singapore

CONTENTS

MIGHTY CARS

Cars have completely changed the modern world. They give people great freedom to travel wherever they want to go and to cover long distances very quickly.

City car

Sports car

About a third of all the cars in the world are in the USA.

TYPES OF CARS

There are lots of different types of cars. City cars are often small and are good for short journeys. They are also easier to park in small spaces. Family cars are more comfortable for long journeys. Hatchbacks have a rear door. Sports cars are small, fast cars that are great fun to drive. Off-roaders, or 'four-by-fours', travel well over muddy, rough ground. Modern supercars are amazingly expensive, fast cars. The mightiest cars of all are racing cars, dragsters and jet-cars that have set speed records.

Saloon car

Four by four

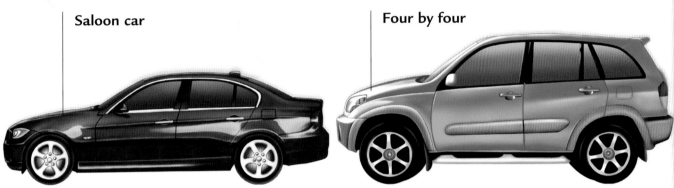

THE NUMBERS GAME

Cars are more popular than ever. There are about 600 million cars on the world's roads today and about 40 million new cars are built every year. There are so many cars that the traffic in big cities often slows to a walking pace, or grinds to a halt altogether. This is called a gridlock.

FAST FACTS
Right or Left
Three-quarters of the world's cars are driven on the right side of the road. Britain, Ireland, Japan, Australia and New Zealand are places where cars drive on the left.

🌐 New cars are shipped around the world and delivered by special transporters.

HOW CARS WORK

Cars are made in different shapes and sizes, but most of them work in the same way. A car is a set of systems that work together.

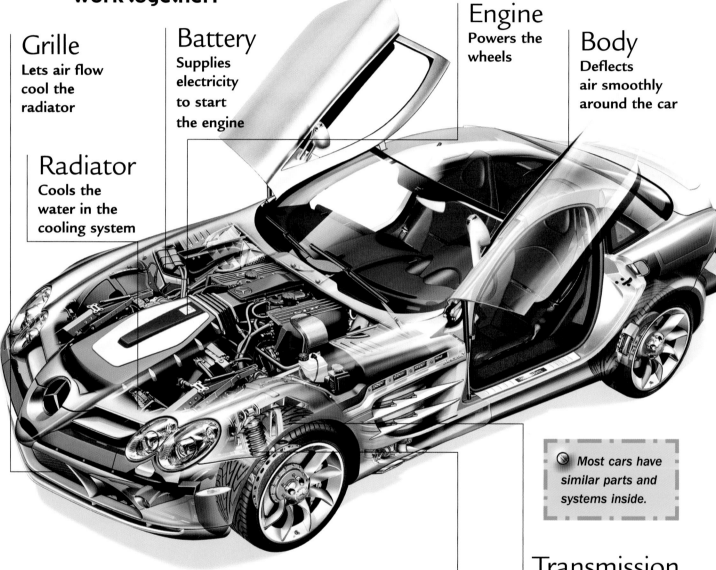

Grille
Lets air flow cool the radiator

Battery
Supplies electricity to start the engine

Engine
Powers the wheels

Body
Deflects air smoothly around the car

Radiator
Cools the water in the cooling system

> Most cars have similar parts and systems inside.

Transmission
Connects the engine to the wheels

Suspension
Gives a smooth ride on bumpy ground

How a Car Works

The fuel system supplies fuel to the engine. The electrical system makes electricity for the engine, lights, radio and other electrical parts. The lubrication system keeps the engine's moving parts covered with slippery oil. The engine drives the wheels.

INTAKE ──────▶ COMPRESSION ──────▶ IGNITION ──────▶ EXHAUST

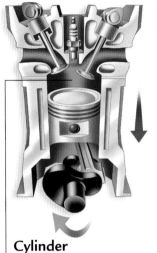
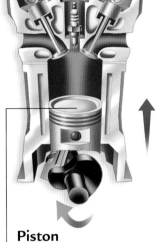
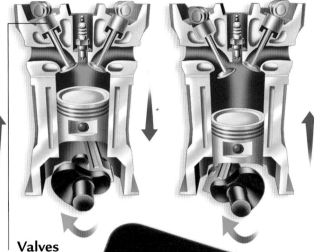

Cylinder   Piston   Valves

Inside a Car Engine

A car engine works by burning fuel inside tubes called cylinders. Most car engines have four, six or eight cylinders. When fuel burns inside a cylinder, the heat makes air in the cylinder expand. The force of expanding air pushes a piston down the cylinder. Pistons moving up and down inside the cylinders provide the power to turn the car's wheels.

FAST FACTS
Waste Products

When a car's engine burns fuel, it produces hot gases. The exhaust system lets these hot gases escape and also makes the engine quieter. In many cars today, the exhaust system cleans up harmful gases before they escape into the air.

THE FIRST CARS

The first road vehicle that moved under its own power was a three-wheel army tractor built more than 230 years ago.

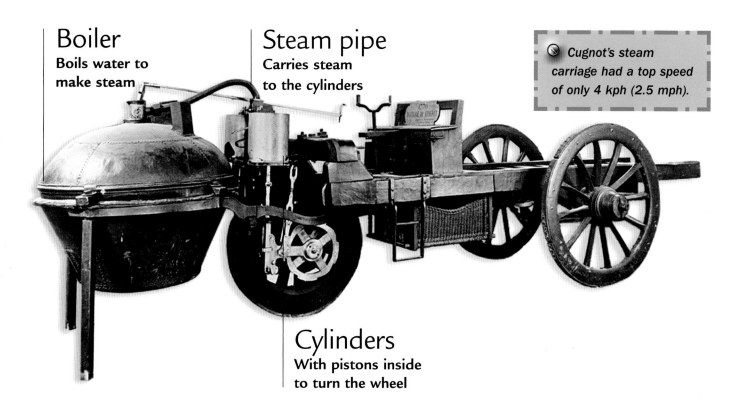

Boiler
Boils water to make steam

Steam pipe
Carries steam to the cylinders

Cugnot's steam carriage had a top speed of only 4 kph (2.5 mph).

Cylinders
With pistons inside to turn the wheel

STEAM POWER

In 1769, a French soldier called Nicolas-Joseph Cugnot built a strange-looking vehicle. It was a three-wheeler with a steam engine. A boiler at the front was filled with water. A fire heated the water and changed it into steam. The steam worked the engine, which turned the front wheel. It could only travel at walking pace, but it showed everyone that road vehicles could move under their own power.

Steam made in the boiler moved pistons up and down inside two cylinders. The pistons turned the front wheel.

> The Benz car had a small petrol engine tucked behind the seat.

FROM STEAM TO PETROL

In 1885, a German engineer called Karl Benz built a new type of car. Its engine worked by burning petrol instead of making steam. It was the first motor car. Steam cars couldn't move until they made enough steam, but petrol cars could get going as soon as their engine started and they didn't need a big boiler full of water.

FAST FACTS

The First Crash

Cugnot crashed one of his tractors into a wall in 1771 and so became the first person to be involved in a vehicle accident!

> In 1886, Gottlieb Daimler fitted a petrol engine to a coach and produced the first four-wheeled car.

Tyres
Pneumatic (air-filled) from the 1890s

CARS FOR ALL

The first cars were very expensive. Only rich people could afford to buy one. But some car makers set out to build cars that everyone could afford to own.

MODEL T

Henry Ford believed that people wanted simple cars that didn't cost much. He was right. In 1908, Ford began making the Model T. In the first year, he sold 10,000 – an amazing number for that time. Over the next 19 years, more than 15 million were produced. The Model T became the most popular car in the world.

Roof
Folds down to the back

Windscreen
Folds down

Wheels
Made of wood with pneumatic (air-filled) tyres

Henry Ford's Model T cost $825 when it went on sale in 1908. By 1926, the price had fallen to only $290.

Body
Available in different styles

Engine
20 horsepower

Starting handle
Turned to start the engine

The Volkswagen Beetle was so popular that it was manufactured for 58 years.

Engine
In the rear

Luggage
Carried at the front

BEETLES AND MINIS

In the 1930s, Ferdinand Porsche designed a simple 'people's car', or Volkswagen, in Germany. It became known as the Beetle because of its shape. More than 21 million Beetles were made. When the Mini appeared in 1959, people were surprised at how tiny it was. However, Minis became so popular that they are still being made today.

---- FAST FACTS
Front-wheel Drive
The Mini's engine powered the front wheels. This was very unusual for the 1950s.

The new Mini is a redesigned and updated version of the hugely popular original Mini.

MIGHTY CARS

BF54 WNE

SUPERCARS

Most cars are made in large numbers to reduce the cost of each one, so that more people can buy them. But some cars are designed to be the best, no matter what the cost. These amazing cars are sometimes called supercars.

BUGATTI VEYRON

The Veyron is the fastest, most powerful and most expensive production car. Its amazing engine and beautiful body shape give it a top speed of about 400 kph (250 mph). As the car speeds up, a wing rises up from the back to keep it steady on the road. A car designed for such high speeds needs special tyres. Its back tyres are the widest on any road car.

Step 1. The rear wing tilts up.

Step 2. The wing rises at higher speeds.

Air scoops
Let in air to cool the brakes

Snorkels
Let air into the engine

Tyres
Created specially for the Veyron

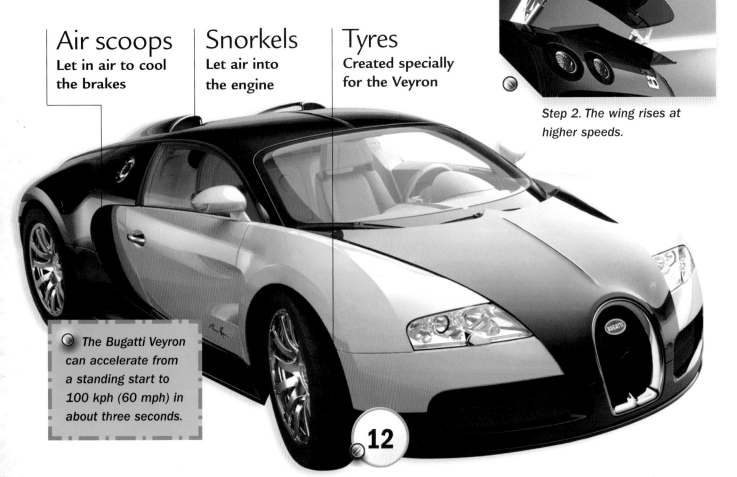

The Bugatti Veyron can accelerate from a standing start to 100 kph (60 mph) in about three seconds.

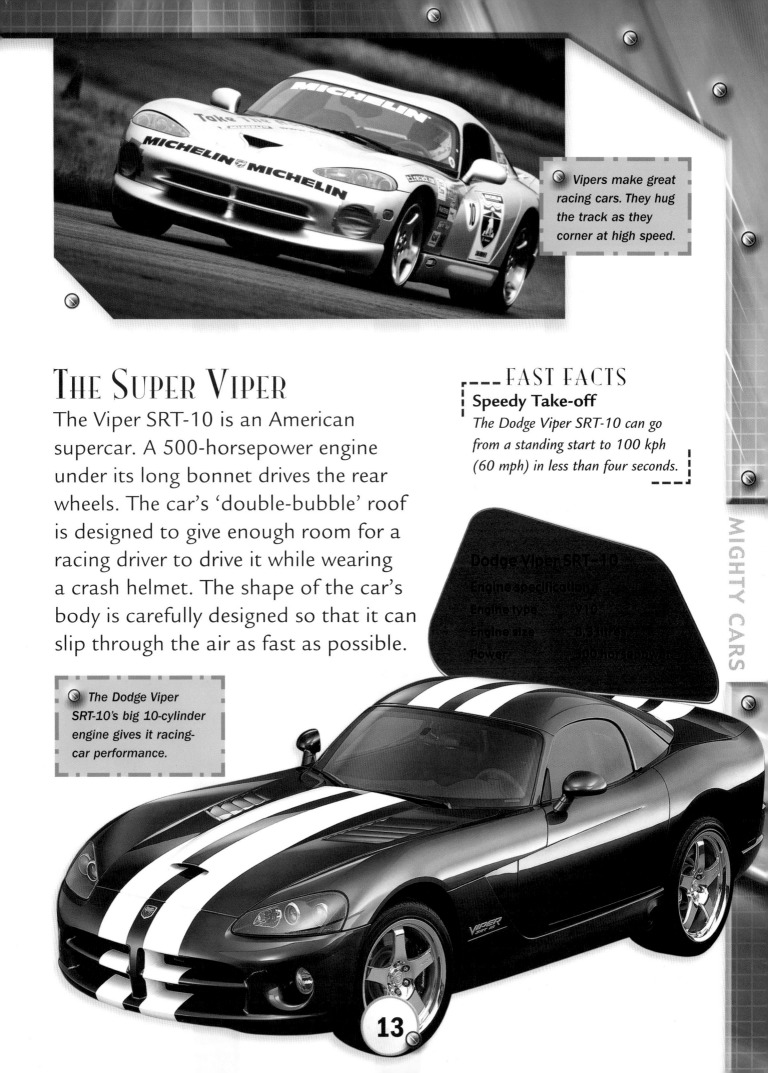

Vipers make great racing cars. They hug the track as they corner at high speed.

THE SUPER VIPER

The Viper SRT-10 is an American supercar. A 500-horsepower engine under its long bonnet drives the rear wheels. The car's 'double-bubble' roof is designed to give enough room for a racing driver to drive it while wearing a crash helmet. The shape of the car's body is carefully designed so that it can slip through the air as fast as possible.

FAST FACTS
Speedy Take-off
The Dodge Viper SRT-10 can go from a standing start to 100 kph (60 mph) in less than four seconds.

Dodge Viper SRT-10
Engine specification
Engine type   V10
Engine size   8.3 litres
Power   500 horsepower

The Dodge Viper SRT-10's big 10-cylinder engine gives it racing-car performance.

MIGHTY CARS

MAKING CARS

Cars used to be built by people, but robots have now taken over a lot of the work. A modern car factory can build a car in less than 20 hours.

PUTTING IT ALL TOGETHER

In the first car factories, each car stayed in one place while workers built it. Henry Ford changed to a faster method. Chains pulled the cars through the factory and workers fitted parts as the cars passed them. Moving assembly lines are still used in car factories, but today many of the workers are robots.

Moving assembly line
To speed up car production

There were few machines on early car production lines. Most of the work was done by hand.

Robots that build cars can use different tools, including mechanical hands to pick things up, drills to cut holes, spray guns for painting and welding tools to join pieces of metal together.

Robots
Weld car bodies together

ROBOTS AT WORK

In a modern car factory, conveyor belts move a long snake of cars through the building. Hundreds of robots build up the car bodies. The robots can lift heavy parts easily and move them to exactly the right place. Robots paint the car bodies, too. However, people are still needed to fit parts such as the seats, controls and windscreens that are too awkward for robots to handle.

FAST FACTS
Robot Car Workers

Nearly half of all the robots in the world work in factories helping to make cars.

15

RACING CARS

Motor-racing is one of the most exciting and popular sports. The fastest racing cars thunder around race-tracks at up to 400 kph (250 mph).

SINGLE SEATERS

Formula 1 cars, Champ cars and Indy Racing League cars are all single-seat racing cars. They are just big enough for the driver to wriggle down inside. Their wings work like upside-down aircraft wings. They press a car down and make its tyres grip the track better so that it can corner faster.

Formula 1 racing car
Engine specification
Engine type   V10
Engine size   3 litres
Power   860 horsepower

Engine
Drives the back wheels

Rear wing
Presses the rear wheels down

Cockpit
The driver's compartment

Body
Made from carbon fibre

Tyres
Made of a soft rubber for maximum grip

Front wing
Pushes the car's nose down

A Formula 1 racing car is built by hand. Each car contains about 10,000 parts.

BURNING UP THE STRIP

Dragsters are cars designed to go as fast as possible down a straight 400 metre (quarter mile) track called a drag strip. Top Fuel Dragsters are the fastest. They accelerate away from the start line faster than a fighter plane or a Formula 1 racing car. They cross the finishing line at nearly 540 kph (335 mph). A whole race may last less than five seconds!

The secret of a Top Fuel Dragster's amazing speed is its 7,000-horsepower engine, as powerful as eight Formula 1 racing cars!

FAST FACTS
NASCAR Racing
American NASCAR racing cars look like ordinary family cars, but each is a hand-built race-car with a top speed of 320 kph (200 mph).

CARS AT WORK

Police cars are packed with equipment to help police officers do their work. The inside of a modern police car can look more like an office than like a car!

POLICE CARS

A standard police car today not only carries a radio, but it also has a computer and video equipment. The crew use all this equipment to contact other officers, check if other cars have been stolen, and even measure the speed of other cars. While a car's speed is checked, a video camera records its picture and its details are downloaded into the police car's computer.

Light bar
Warns drivers that a police car is approaching

Body
A standard production car body

Police cars are filled with computer and communications equipment.

Grille
May conceal video camera and radar speed detector

Computer
Displays information about crimes

Radio
Lets the crew talk to other officers

CARS AT WAR

Wherever American soldiers go, their Hummers go too. The Hummer, or High Mobility Multipurpose Wheeled Vehicle (HMMWV), is a small truck, but soldiers use it like a car to get around because it's a tough vehicle with enough room inside for four fully equipped soldiers.

A police car driver is surrounded by scores of buttons and switches that control all the extra equipment the car carries.

FAST FACTS
Electric Cars
The first police cars in the 1890s were powered by electricity because there were very few cars with petrol engines.

The Hummer has lots of space underneath so that it can travel over rough ground.

CUSTOM CARS

Most cars are built in large numbers and each car is the same as thousands of others. Some people want their cars to be different from other cars. Making a car different is called customising and the cars are called custom cars.

HOT RODS

All custom cars are designed to look cool. Some are designed to be powerful and fast, too. These custom cars are also called hot rods. Most custom cars begin as a family car. Its shape is changed, a new engine put in, and an eye-catching design painted on.

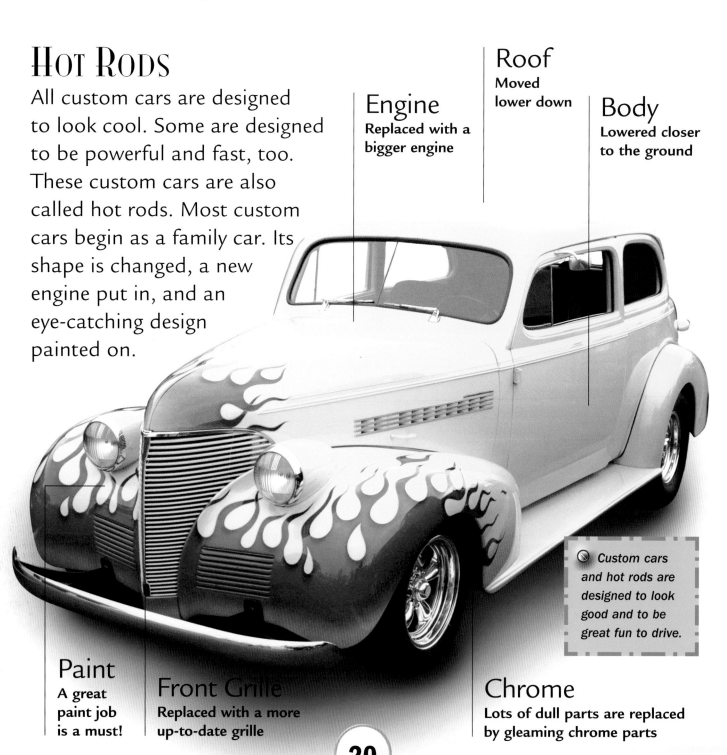

Engine
Replaced with a bigger engine

Roof
Moved lower down

Body
Lowered closer to the ground

Paint
A great paint job is a must!

Front Grille
Replaced with a more up-to-date grille

Chrome
Lots of dull parts are replaced by gleaming chrome parts

Custom cars and hot rods are designed to look good and to be great fun to drive.

> Stretch limos are luxurious inside. There's plenty of room for big, comfortable seats, television sets, DVD players and sound systems.

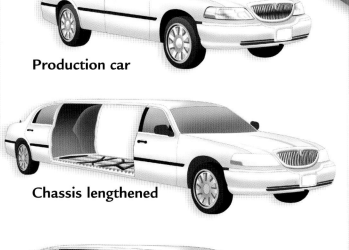

Production car

Chassis lengthened

Structure strengthened

Body rebuilt

STRETCH LIMOS

An extreme way to customise a car is to cut it in half and make it longer. The front and back of the car are pulled apart and an extra section is put in the middle. The finished car can be up to 3 metres longer! A car customised like this is called a stretched limousine, or stretch limo. Stretch limos are used for special journeys or events.

> A stretch limo needs a super-strong chassis, or frame, underneath to stop it sagging in the middle!

FAST FACTS
History of Flame Painting

Flame painting first started in California in the late 1940s. Today, subtle flames, screaming flames, and tribal and traditional flames are a popular part of hot rods.

VIP SPECIALS

Presidents, royalty and other Very Important People (VIPs) often travel in large, luxury cars. However, these are not ordinary luxury vehicles. These cars are specially built to protect their passengers from attack.

ARMOURED CARS

The cars that carry the most important people have an armoured body and bullet-proof glass to protect against gunfire and small bombs. The window glass can be more than 6 centimetres thick! The engine is armoured too, so that the driver can keep the car moving and drive away from danger.

The US President travels in safety in a Cadillac deVille with top secret armour and other special defences.

Windows
Made from bullet-proof glass

Run-flat tyres
Work even with holes in them

Satellite tracker
Finds the car if it is stolen or hijacked

Night vision
Lets the driver see in the dark

Body
Lined with bullet-proof armour

Fuel tank
Stops the fuel from exploding

An armoured limousine undergoes a fiery test.

TESTING TIMES

The makers of armoured cars know how well they work because they test the cars. No other cars are put through tests as tough as this. Armoured cars are tested by shooting at them and blowing them up to make sure they really do protect their important passengers!

FAST FACTS

Gas Attack!

The most expensive armoured VIP cars have air-tight doors and windows to protect the driver and passengers against chemical and biological attacks.

23

MODERN CARS

Cars have changed a lot since the Benz three-wheeler in 1885. Modern cars are bigger, heavier, more powerful, faster, more comfortable, more reliable and safer, too.

SAFETY FIRST

Modern cars are safer than old cars because they are thoroughly tested. They are deliberately crashed to check how strong they are. Special mechanical people, called crash test dummies, sit in the cars to show what would happen to real people in a crash.

Crash tests
Check how strong cars are

Crash testing makes sure that cars are strong enough to protect people inside and to show up any weak spots in a car.

Instruments
In the car send information to computers

Damage
Filmed by high-speed cameras

BELT UP!

Modern cars have lots of safety features and electronic aids. Anti-lock brakes stop them quickly without skidding. Seat belts hold the driver and passengers tightly in their seats. Air bags blow up to cushion the impact of a crash. Satellite navigation systems help drivers to find their way.

A car's air bag bursts out at up to 320 kph (200 mph). It has to work this fast so that it's fully inflated before the driver's head hits the steering wheel.

FAST FACTS
Crash testing cars began in the USA in the 1950s. It was soon being used in many other countries by car manufacturers.

A car's navigation system works out exactly where the car is by receiving radio signals from satellites in space.

RECORD BREAKERS

The fastest cars in the world have jet engines! They are cars built to set the fastest of all the car speed records – the land speed record.

FASTER THAN SOUND

On October 15, 1997, a car called Thrust SSC crossed the Black Rock Desert in the USA faster than a Jumbo Jet airliner! SSC stands for supersonic car, because Thrust SSC was designed to go faster than the speed of sound.

Engines
Two Rolls-Royce Spey 205 jet engines

Thrust SSC is as powerful as about 116 Formula 1 racing cars!

Parachutes
Help to stop the car

Cockpit
Houses the driver, fighter pilot Andy Green

Wheels
Made from solid aluminium

Chassis
Frame made from welded steel tubes

Nose cone
Sharp to punch through the air

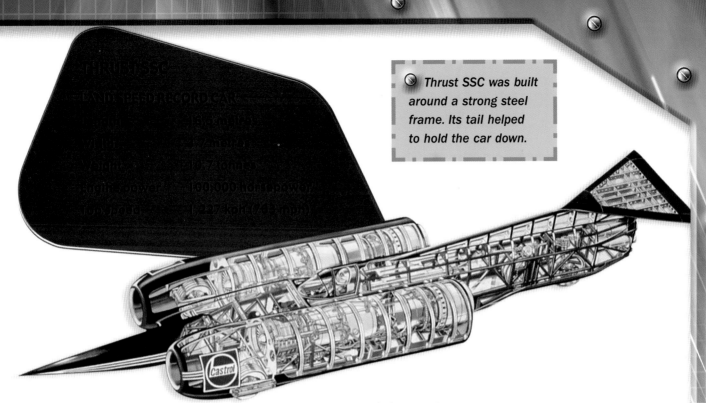

Thrust SSC was built around a strong steel frame. Its tail helped to hold the car down.

SETTING THE RECORD

To set the record, Thrust SSC had to drive along a course in the desert faster than the speed of sound, then turn around and do it again in the opposite direction, all within one hour! A car going as fast as Thrust SSC is not easy to stop. Brakes alone won't work. Thrust SSC shot parachutes out behind it to help slow it down.

FAST FACTS
Electric Record
The first land speed record was set on December 8, 1898, in France. It was set by an electric car that reached the amazing speed, for that time, of 63 kph (39 mph).

Spirit of America – Sonic Arrow challenged Thrust SSC for the land speed record in 1997. Its driver, Craig Breedlove, sat in the car's nose in front of a fighter-plane's jet engine.

27

FUTURE CARS

Future cars will probably be kinder to the environment. They will have cleaner engines, or no engines at all. Some of them may even be able to fly.

FLYING CARS

Cinema films set in the future sometimes show cars that can fly. Well, some flying cars have already been built! The Moller Skycar is powered by four pods with fans inside. The fans are driven by eight engines. The jets of air from the fans can be sent in different directions to steer the car in the air.

> *The Skycar's engines burn the same petrol that cars use, so the Skycar can land at an ordinary fuel station to fill up.*

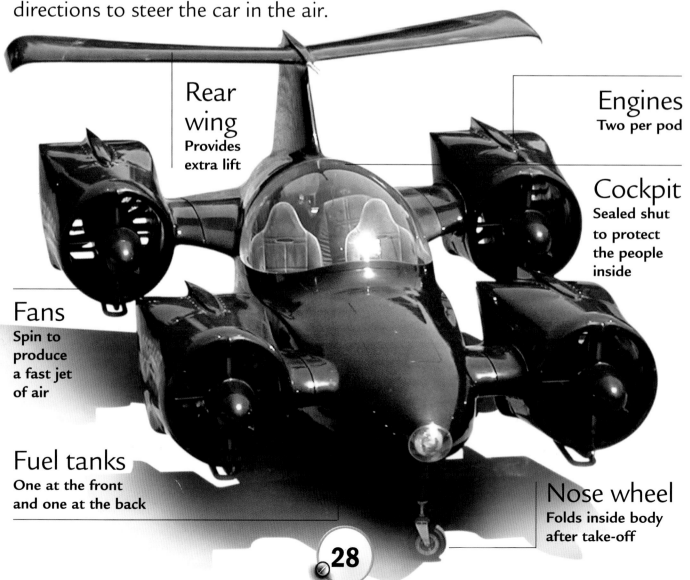

Rear wing
Provides extra lift

Engines
Two per pod

Cockpit
Sealed shut to protect the people inside

Fans
Spin to produce a fast jet of air

Fuel tanks
One at the front and one at the back

Nose wheel
Folds inside body after take-off

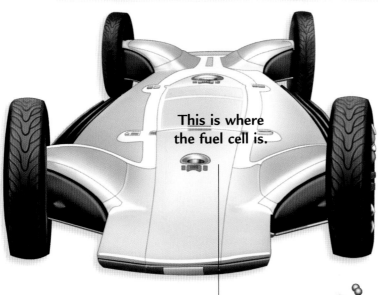

This is where the fuel cell is.

Cars like the General Motors Hy-Wire cut air pollution because their fuel cells are cleaner than car engines today.

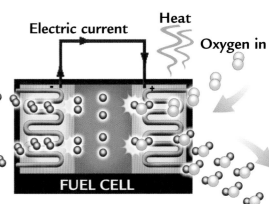

Electric current

Heat

Oxygen in

Hydrogen in

FUEL CELL

Water out

FUEL CELLS

Some future cars may have no engine! Instead, they might be powered by fuel cells. A fuel cell is a device that makes electricity from chemicals. Fuel cells are being used by some spacecraft and fuel cell cars have already been built. The General Motors Hy-Wire is a fuel cell car.

FAST FACTS
Shuttle Power
The Space Shuttle uses fuel cells to make electricity and drinking water.

TIMELINE

BF54 WNE

1769
The first self-propelled vehicle is built by Nicolas Cugnot.

1865
The Red Flag Act forces British drivers to have a man walking in front of their vehicle waving a red flag for safety!

1885
Karl Benz builds the first successful motor car.

1886
Gottlieb Daimler designs the first modern petrol engine.

1893
Benz builds his first four-wheel car.

1893
The first car number plates are introduced in France.

1896
Electric cars are introduced.

1898
The first land speed record, 63 kph (39 mph), is set by an electric car.

1899
The world's first self-propelled police vehicle, an electric car, is used in Akron, Ohio, USA.

1900
Nearly half of the world's cars are electric.

1904
The first purpose-built taxis are equipped with a meter for measuring distance and speed.

1908
The Ford Model T is introduced.

1910
The first police motor car, a Model T Ford, starts work in Akron, Ohio, USA.

1916
More than half of the world's cars are Model T Fords.

1916
Cars with windscreen wipers are introduced in the USA.

1927
The last Model T Ford is produced.

1938
The Volkswagen Beetle is introduced.

1951
Chrysler introduces power steering in cars.

1959
The Mini car is introduced.

1962
The first robots are installed in a car factory in the USA.

1997
First supersonic land speed record set by Thrust SSC.

1998
The VW New Beetle is introduced.

2002
There are more than 530 million cars in the world.

2003
The last of the original VW Beetles is manufactured.

2003
Drivers have to pay to bring their cars into central London.

GLOSSARY

assembly line

The part of a car factory where cars are put together.

crash test dummy

A mechanical model of a person used for car safety tests.

cylinder

One of the tube-shaped parts inside a car engine where the fuel is burned.

exhaust

The gases that come out of an engine when fuel is burned.

fuel

A liquid such as petrol that is burned inside a car engine to provide the energy to turn the car's wheels.

hatchback

A car with an extra door in the back.

horsepower

A unit used to measure the power of a car's engine. A small car might have an engine of about 100 horsepower.

hot rod

A customised car that has been rebuilt and repainted to be fast, good-looking and fun to drive.

lubrication

Covering the moving parts of a car's engine with oil so that they slide over each other easily.

off-roader

A car designed to work well on soft muddy ground. Also called a four-by-four, because all four of its wheels are driven by the engine.

radiator

Part of a car's engine that cools the water or oil inside it by letting air blow around it and carry the heat away.

sports car

A small car designed to be fast, sleek and great fun to drive.

stretch limo

A luxury car that has been rebuilt with an extra section in the middle to make it longer.

supercar

A very expensive, powerful and fast car.

suspension

The springs and other parts of a car that let it move along smoothly while the wheels go up and down over bumps.

transmission

The gears and other parts of a car that connect the engine to the wheels.

V8

A popular type of car engine. It has eight cylinders in two rows of four connected together at the bottom, to make the shape of a letter V.

31

INDEX

WEBFINDER

http://suzy.co.nz/suzysworld/Factpage.asp?FactSheet=256   *Car facts, experiments and jokes!*

http://www.nhra.com/streetlegal/whatisadragrace.html   *Find out about drag racing*

http://www.nhra.com/streetlegal/funfacts.html   *Lots of fun facts about drag racing*

http://www.scapca.org/cool_car_facts.asp   *Cool facts about cars with cleaner engines*

http://www.indyracing.com/indycar/garage/facts.php   *Lots of fun facts about motor racing*

http://www.howstuffworks.com/nascar   *Find out about NASCAR racing cars*

http://www.wsc.org.au   *Visit this website to learn about racing cars powered by sunshine!*

http://www.guinnessworldrecords.com   *Use this website to find out about record-breaking cars*